SAKURA PARK

Sakura Park

Poems

Rachel Wetzsteon

A Karen & Michael Braziller Book
PERSEA BOOKS / NEW YORK

    Persea Books, Inc.
    853 Broadway
    New York, NY 10003

Library of Congress Cataloging-in-Publication Data
Wetzsteon, Rachel
    Sakura Park : poems / Rachel Wetzsteon.
        p. cm.
    Poems.
    "A Karen & Michael Braziller book."
    ISBN 0-89255-324-3 (original trade pbk. : alk. paper)
        I. Title.

PS3573.E945S25 2006
811'.54–dc22   2005034207

Designed by Lytton Smith
First Edition
Printed in the United States of America

Acknowledgments

I'm grateful to the editors of the following journals in which some of the poems in this collection first appeared, occasionally in different form:

Barrow Street: "Rosalind in Manhattan"

Literary Imagination: "On Irony"

The Nation: "Pemberley," "Short Ode to Screwball Women"

The New Republic: "Thirty-Three" (x)

The New Yorker: "Lawyers on the Left Bank," "Love and Work"

Open City: "Gusts," "Largo"

The Paris Review: "Homage to Eddie Izzard"

Parnassus: "Ruskin's Whip"

Pequod: "Notes Toward a Definition of the Self"

Poetry: "On Leaving the Bachelorette Brunch," "Sakura Park"

Poetry Review (UK): "Thirty-Three" (i)

Poets.org: "At the Zen Mountain Monastery"

Raritan: "Cloud Studies (I)," "Short Ode to Morningside Heights"

Rattapallax: "Flaneur Haiku"

Salmagundi: "Little Song for a Big Night"

Southwest Review: "A Day at the Revival House"

Threepenny Review: "Madeleine for Awhile"

The Yale Review: "Manhattan Triptych," "Umbrella Weather"

Zone 3: "Apologies to an Ambulance," "Moonlight and Love Songs"

Thanks to the editors of these collections:

"And This Time I Mean It," "Blue Octavo Haiku," and "Commands for the End of Summer" appeared in *Bright Pages: Yale Writers 1701-2001*, edited by J.D. McClatchy (Yale University Press, 2001).

"A Trampoline in Wayne" appeared in *110 Stories: New York Writes after September 11*, edited by Ulrich Baer (New York University Press, 2002).

"Autumn Ghazal" was published in *Ravishing DisUnities: Real Ghazals in English*, edited by Agha Shahid Ali (Wesleyan University Press, 2000).

"Spring (The Procession)" was commissioned for the exhibit "A Gallery of Poems" at the Yale University Art Gallery and published in *Words for Images: A Gallery of Poems*, edited by John Hollander and Joanna Weber (Yale University Press, 2001).

I'd also like to express my boundless gratitude to the American Academy of Arts and Letters, Gabe Fried, the MacDowell Colony, Lytton Smith, William Paterson University, and the Corporation of Yaddo, without whose good faith and generosity this book never could have been written.

Contents

ↄ

"Not to find one's way in a city may well be uninteresting and banal. It requires ignorance—nothing more. But to lose oneself in a city—as one loses oneself in a forest—that calls for quite a different schooling. Then, signboard and street names, passers-by, roofs, kiosks, or bars must speak to the wanderer like a crackling twig under his feet in the forest."

—Walter Benjamin

"One does not care for girls till they are grown up."

—Jane Austen, *Letters*

"I'm having a rhetorical conversation!"

—Max Bialystock, *The Producers*

Sunrise over Low

This view is new: gray dome set in a pink sky
like a gem in a ring, rooftops confirming

levels attained, and plump watertowers
perching on each one, my trusty protectors.

It seemed I would not flee old haunts so much
as rise above them, snug in penthouse wisdom.

But daybreak springs its surprises like a shy face
after a drink too many: the dome rebukes me

for spines not cracked, and the banners of dawn
are teases, are sorrows, are prizes, are hunters.

(Once I took a vacation from my vocation.
Getting out of bed was never so easy

yet the sunrise suffered so: where were the clouds
like camels, the fresh day's difficult red riddles?)

The morning rouses itself into gorgeous disquiet.
And as I head out to meet it, run wild,

you Birnam wood of watertowers, you raw sky
trying on colors like a girl before a dance.

Short Ode to Morningside Heights

Convergence of worlds, old stomping ground,
comfort me in my dark apartment
when my latest complaint shrinks my focus
to a point so small it's hugely present
but barely there, and I fill the air
with all the spiteful words I spared the streets.

The pastry shop's abuzz
with crazy George and filthy graffiti,
but the peacocks are strutting across the way
and the sumptuous cathedral gives
the open-air banter a reason to deepen:
build structures inside the mind, it tells
the languorous talkers, to rival the ones outside!

Things are and are not solid.
As Opera Night starts at Caffé Taci,
shapes hurry home with little red bags,
but do they watch the movies they hold
or do they forego movies for rooftops
where they catch Low's floating dome in the act
of always being about to fly away?

Ranters, racers, help me remember
that the moon-faced fountain's the work of many hands,
that people linger at Toast long after we've left.
And as two parks frame the neighborhood—

green framing gray and space calming clamor—
be for me, well-worn streets, a context
I can't help carrying home, a night fugue
streaming over my one-note *how, when, why*.
Be the rain for my barren indoor cry.

Little Song for a Big Night

What pure thought cannot contemplate
bent body understands;
why not kill time obeying its
crude, casual demands?
   Wake, limbs, wake
    beneath his knowing hands.

The conscience, high and mighty, says
All right, if you insist;
the convict, deeper down, records
the places he has kissed.
   Roll, parts, roll;
    make up for thrills you missed.

The harmless pleasure somehow leaves
a festering red sore;
the heart grows fond, the lust is just
as violent as before.
   Race, thoughts, race
    when healthy fun cries *More*.

The body is nostalgic for
the dimple and the shin;
the soul is over in the wood
looking for its twin.
   Feel, fool, feel
    the double hell begin.

When one night hurries to a close
a residue remains;
romantics cannot separate
vast sighs from little stains.
  Sink, heart, sink
    into your latest chains.

Infidels

i.

It all came down to whether life
could change in a shattering instant,
slow clouds you saw as pillows becoming
restless and bumpy shapes outside your house.

Fair dweller, I would change your mind;
I bring you poppies, lilacs, riotous blooms.
But you place them all in a tasteful gray vase
and the beads of moisture only stiffen the ring.

ii.

Supposing, though, I roamed your house
with customized rings on my phone and finger,
watching the red wine in my glass
turn slowly into lukewarm water,

envying clouds their verve and purpose?
Smother me with pillows, I'd cry; I died
long ago. Game over: the threshold's
bitter cold, and just where I want to be.

Saturday Night

Rain all day, and a rattle of windows
keeps the self and its secrets inside.

But weather only seals the matter;
islands are just as large in sunlight.

They are gathering around me tonight,
the necessary, the difficult deaths.

If I cast away one kind of worry—
moods too blue and hair too wayward—

there would still be fear of the moment
in which a secret becomes a statement,

the statement, sneeze-like, leaves the body
and the soul, unblessed and quite as normal

as any other, enters a world
of seesaws, free will, and watercooler rumor.

I hoard excuses like coins, but at least
I've reached a point where I can say

the frisson was fun, the kiss would be better;
the noise in my room is the sounding brass

and tinkling cymbal of a weary one-girl band.
If not tomorrow, then soon, then soon,

something will sink in other than rain:
when crowds spill onto the plaza after the opera,

they carry the music with them as they mingle
(meet me by the fountain) under the stars.

About Time

i.

I loitered with intent as the sun went down
and when that got me nowhere, I loitered
in a cloud of apathy as it came up again.
Days passed like sedated madmen—
pleasant, benign, but without that shifty
look in the eyes that lets you know
that at any moment anything might happen.
All times were alike and no times mattered,
all of which was a sure sign that
democracy is good for the world
but ruinous to the heart: when you look
at a clock without the furious urge
to set the hour hand forward or back,
you might as well be signing your will;
your feet may be running, but your pulse is standing still.

ii.

Not that I knew it at the time.
It took a sudden entrance to show me
the hours I had wasted
thinking all hours were the same;
I'd still be sleeping if I hadn't seen
the face that held the future
as it summoned up the past.
I was crossing off the days when the moment imploded.

iii.

Eyes met, sparks flew, watches melted,
and then the shrill bells rang again,
their citywide harangue
sending us home before our time.
But now that I have a night to recall
and another to await, how strange it seems
that a minute ago I was barely alive,
and if I could place the hours in a line-up
I'd say that one was harmless, that one was clever,
that one was friendly but nothing special,
but that one there, the tall one with glasses,
that one I remember well:
it crept up fast and departed too soon
and until it returns to the scene of the crime
the clock face is my jailer,
the voiceless wind my best friend;
I'll spend my days revisiting
the streets I always thought were gray,
I'll spend my nights imagining
the pleasures that will come to me in good time.

And This Time I Mean It

All over the city, people are crying
crocodile tears that dry up before the cause
of weeping crosses the street; interns say great things
about the men who got them their jobs
then roll their eyes when the coast is clear. Appearing
as a way of keeping foes and bosses happy,
the habit fastens and takes hold
until it starts occurring
even among friends, so that only
with effort can the banter be decoded:
"I'll be there" means "Never will I budge";
"No" is a subtle way of saying "Sure."

Raised in a place where the worst that can happen
happens every day, I also had a habit
of opening a gap between the mind thinking
and the mouth expressing; only by throwing
intricate veils over what I meant
could I reach the nearest corner
without crying out for merciful armfuls
of coins, seeing eye dogs, golden syringes dropped
from the sky. Soon, though, I wondered whether
there were two of me living in one house:
one who did the breathing
and one, all smirks and eyebrows, who cracked the jokes.
Now I suffer from other problems
but this one's gone for good. Before we met
I hovered above my feelings

like a singer above a low and difficult note
or a dandy suspended in a balloon
over a plague-ridden village. But if my old friends
waved to me on my armored cloud,
a handshake with a new one took me
down, toward the street's precise rough music,
down toward terror and truth.

A Game of Tag

Street noise, ugly and menacing,
streams through the booth and tries to drown out
my latest message. Let it.
I called from an outdoor phone, though only
blocks away from home, for just that reason.
And when, aimless in your apartment,
you're suddenly moved to call me back
and I screen you from the couch, too scared to speak,
I'll savor every sound in the background
although it makes your message that much
harder to hear. And will I return the call
when I'm certain, not only that you're not home,
but also that my room has grown
as wild as it ever will, steampipes clanging
like angry hammers, God only knows
what deafening things going on
outside my window? Without a scruple,
with every hope that chance and plumbing
cancel my cowardice, declare my love.
Talking over all this noise
is not a struggle to make myself heard
as much as a way of *being* heard, engines shouting
what I keep hidden, sad dogs baying
my little lungs out, every single obstacle showing
the pleasures of a game of tag
in the world's loudest city: there's storm, there's stress
and it's hard as hell to hear myself think,
but only because a greater hell

encircles me wherever I stand,
turning a minute in a booth
into a roar of sirens, traffic, absence—
a sweet confusion unknown to lovers
soundly asleep in the still of the silent night.

A Bluff

Looking down at the city below,
I am almost grateful that when I said
I have met my soul, my soul said no;
it was a verdict that nearly bled

the hope from my veins, but it got me thinking.
They get what they want and they never
want it again; that's tragic. But as the blinking
outer boroughs' houses warn me, whatever

sprouted from our encounter would only
have turned my fierce questions on this lookout
where all seems possible—how will a grown me
talk, dress, kiss?—to jeering answers: cookout

our one flame; icebox leaking; the bureau top's
skyline of unguents a nightly reminder
that when the hunt for passion stops
another sort of journey begins, kinder,

gentler, slower, and thoroughly boring.
(*Ah*, Beauty pleaded, *Give me back my Beast.*)
I cry all the time; I hate the ghouls snoring
next to the people they love. But at least

I won't be someone who, smiling too often,
gives too much away; your shipwrecked
wandering stare won't cruelly soften
into the landlocked glare of wan respect.

Down below a strangled voice cries, *Is
the hemlock pie ready?* But here on the bluff
the city's radiant with surprises,
too much of a good thing is never enough.

Moonlight and Love Songs

"I cannot choose the time
for my journey,
I must find my own way
in this darkness."
—Wilhelm Müller, *Die Winterreise*

That walk I took last night
from my part of town to yours and back:
was it a proof of music's power
or a further sign that wrecks with headwounds

should stay inside? That song I hummed
as I trotted along—the one about the person
who walked all night—did it alter what I saw?
These days it's hard to tell a sound from an echo.

Troops gather in a chamber of mirrors
and snicker wildly as they unveil
another mirror, thugs prowl the city
putting quotes around the pairs of initials

that linger faintly on ancient trees,
and maiden speeches always feel musty
however well they get delivered,
however hard the phrases try

to make it on their own. But slippery as
my foothold felt as I crept past your house,
there is a difference between a void
and a vaulted hall where shouts and murmurs

cross and recross like beams of light. Last night
as a blue moon soothed the sleeping city
the weight of the past caressed it also:
I found a green ribbon in a gutter

and though no hunter trailed me, I swear I saw
three girls in tee shirts with painted arrows,
I met an organ grinder, and now that I'm home
I know that these feet I soak in a bowl

are mine, are mine (even if my love
annoyingly isn't), but that this journey
is only one chapter of a story
of crowds who set out, singing songs, in winter.

But for the Grace

My crazy friend across the country
calls to tell me about her year: the jerk
who loved and left her, the way she stubbornly
went on adoring, and the slow hard work

it took just to drag herself out of bed
in the morning, until now, high on pills
with space-creature names, finally persuaded
he's really gone, sad raconteur who fills

wide ears with wicked stories, she's getting by.
I let her rave for hours, thinking, Rough
break, poor kid, but get over it! But who am I
to criticize? Her tale's my own, though I'm private enough

to wrap my secrets in veils of frilly
banter, thick webs of gauzy bravado. Later I'll tell
her story to friends and we'll agree
she's cracked past mending. One person's hell

is another's anecdotal heaven. Yet even so I'll be faking
most of my enjoyment. I used to believe
that growing up meant violently taking
a messy heart from a clean white sleeve

and shoving the redness deeper in
where, far from the vulgar public's eye,
safe under layers of leathery skin,
it bled discreetly. But lately I'm struck by

the dignity of full disclosure, the glory of loud,
mad lovers who lay their lives on the line
and carry their hearts through the scandalized crowd
crying, Like it or not, this mangled thing is mine.

Apologies to an Ambulance

The red light was my racing heart,
the siren my pain made public,
and the body inside, a study in scarlet,
was battered yet somehow grotesquely pretty.
I drew a rosy curtain over the city.
But the naked city went on bleeding, and so
to the ambulance that roars down my street
apologies, and to the wretch in the back
apologies too: you come from a place
where pulp's not fiction, you know a world
where bullets are more than metaphors
for lovely eyes, and though I roped you
into my story I'll let you go now, wish you
safe passage through a lifetime of green lights.

Evening News

The former lovers sit in a café
   while the day
comes to a sweetly melancholy end;
a good companion makes a better friend
and huddled over coffee cups and plates
they talk of faded passion and new dates
in tones as soft, as gentle and as blue
   as the view.

I always thought the sequel to a kiss
   went like this—
you left all fair and cloudy times behind
and never stopped to sob or change your mind;
you viewed rough seas from a safe ledge above.
The boundary dividing like and love
was made of strong materials, I thought,
   but it's not.

As puffs of smoke, released into the air,
   linger there
and form an intermediary screen
between your eyes and faces they've just seen,
feelings live on, and when my late mate blurts
"I'm seeing someone," how the sentence hurts,
and when my head concludes that all are heels,
   how it reels.

Before this wholly unexpected blast
    from the past
I thought I'd fallen into seas so deep
that nothing else could ever make me weep;
I thought I'd buried my dead love for good
in an abandoned, dusty neighborhood.
But I soon learned that corpses can survive,
    half alive.

So bluster, wind, and smile, sophisticate;
    I've been hit
with tons and tons of strangely heavy bricks,
I feel the brute force of a million kicks
but I have never felt less well or wise.
Perhaps some unborn demon will devise
a hotter fury or a crueler one;
    hell has none.

Umbrella Weather

To be drawn out of doors by the first sign
of rain on the window, to be happier drenched
than dry, to go out in weather
that others come in from, warrants a stare
from passing faces, and I know what it means:
there goes someone with serious problems.
Problems I have, and a nasty stammer to prove it.
But when I run into streets that are shiny,
my love of the downpour doesn't mean
I'm courting sorrow, or getting sick on purpose.
Umbrella weather, though people who flee
seem not to know it, soothes wounds
by making them bigger:
if pain must come, it might as well be
dripping on bricks and blowing through trees
rather than staying in and turning paler.
None of this happens in calmer weather.
To be sobbing in sunlight, groaning on dry land
always leaves me feeling as if
I'm foreign, I'm freakish, I'm out of the loop
until a storm comes and I'm in it again
only deeper now, with a smile no news can ruin.
I throw up a curse and it comes back a blessing;
I look around and my love is pouring
all over the city—crude sighs, small tears
are larger and finer than they first appear
when they come rampaging down, as wind and as rain.

Radishes

I have had my share of black moods
and feeling blue; I have seen red
until flames licked the hems of sweaters;
but today—eternal return of the not same!—
my head became a radish
planted by banter
and watered by wry asides.
You could lay me on a plate
and frugally dine; I'd like to be
so consumed; but better still
was the sweet surprise (our roots tell truths)
of another radish swelling by my side.
With two deep secrets spilling themselves,
with these red faces, the wonderful garden grows.

Snow Day

Blizzard conditions
kept me from sharing my day
with you in person:

the Philip K. Dick
novel I consumed like cake;
the forest of flakes

outside my window;
my ardent guilty smoking—
I loved them alone

but I'm no good as
a woman in white; the self's
relational, needs

others to keep it
warm! Past the deep snowdrifts, from
the heart of the storm,

in this silent room,
hear me holler my stories
across the Hudson.

Six Leagues Under

Unlike the sharks who, if they want
to stay alive must stay in motion,
some prey upon the very young
in the deep folds of the ocean.

I'd sat upon the beach so long
that even the lifeguard, bored ingrate,
fell asleep thinking doubtful starfish
and skittish crabs were my dry fate.

But suddenly I've plunged into water
without wading or warning to guide me in.
You prick me, I bleed and am so madly happy,
but now comes the wait for the terrible fin.

Seeing Red

Day after day, like a visiting general
inspecting sluggish troops or a scholar hot
on a dead man's trail, I passed the rows of flowers
bundled into bouquets outside the store

where people make their own salads, observing how
the petals of fancy breeds fell sooner
than those of plainer ones, noting that
the bundles would form a spectrum ranging

from dusty pink to deepest scarlet
if I lined them up in proper order, until one day,
dragging my frail brain—and along with it a heart
made frailer too by a recent,

remarkable turn of events—past the store,
I knew that for all the faculties a sudden,
unexpected blow to the head takes away (skill
at ranking petals vanished, names of colors spun

like leaves in my brain's windy lobes), there is one great thing
it gives and gives: the candor to be able to say,
at the scene of a red and fragrant chaos,
in a low voice choked with wonder, These are roses.

Glosa

O rose, thou art sick.
The invisible worm
that flies in the night
in the howling storm

has found her flower, has struck gold.
(Cloud nine had me at sixes and sevens
but swans, I noted, mate for life.)
O rose, thou art sick

with vanishing fever, and said Hello,
I must be going, I crave cavorting
in neon-streaked puddles with
the invisible worm.

I see my arms outstretched on the bed
but when, wormlike, I burrow deeper
there's no one there: O briefest of joys
that flies in the night

you have flung my self away from me too;
it still clings helplessly to you
in the vases of strangers,
in the howling storm.

Seventh Sunday

Since you were not Hume's sunrise
I watch the late-May moonrise alone

and a nicotine trance assures me
that summer is coming, and the arrival

of painted toenails; that at last
I truly understand aubades

and James Stewart's vacant hospital gaze
after his wits have vanished with his love;

that the transmigration of bruises
from skin to spirit brings about

such splendid depths of character
you'll drop a dime and never hear a sound.

Clouds race across the moon's pale face.
I have character to spare, it is

no comfort; I will write us down,
making nothing happen, it won't repair

this ache of failed induction, these eyes
that live for sunlight, though the sky stays dark.

After Eden

Somewhere Zeno was smiling, the foul
goblins of paradox were wearing
their fairest clothes that night. My Dinner
with a Chainsaw, the evening could have
been called; and when one too many led
to wise judgments too few, "I'm trying
to break up with you!" he shouted as
stockings and scruples flew; and what was
over wasn't; the brutal doings
were sweeter than a caress; the thrill
of it happening and the horror
of it being an awful mistake
collided like sweaty bodies in
the dark, disheveled room. So this is
moving on, she reflected after
he left. But what was motion? No straight
bright line but a wind every bit as
stormy as the people it carried
away from safety, through towns that froze
and burned, helping them forward but not
letting them forget for a second
their ceaseless looking for what is lost,
their sad resemblance to the quick and
stubborn arrows that never arrive.

Thought Experiments in Early June

I called my spies, but my spies were engaged,
shouted into the phone what I already
knew: fact-finding was a sad
and pointless business. Dress as a tree
and see the pair emerging; trace whereabouts,
socks bought—it was pursuit too late,
a flashlight revealing a bolted door.

I summoned my inner harlot and gave her
weapons? resources? One or the other:
a wine glass that was never empty,
a mind that always was. And yet
she disobeyed my sternest instructions
to kiss and forget—the wonder of those
curbside conversions! She grew fond.

I thought of galaxies, icy realms
where the mess and the bother, the frantic bodies
in trenchcoats and see-through cocktail dresses
were pindots. I thought until it hurt.
But cathedral bells outside my window
still turned into mourners every hour
and then silence, not thinking, filled the air.

Two Cheers

See me gather the spoils: a sharpened nose
for the foul ways of humans; a ledger full of scary
bedtime stories; a sorrow which,
converted to rage, could light a whole small town.
Watch me lift a brimming glass and drink
to grudges, bitter insights, poisoned wells.
But what's gone wrong? My lips, too pinched
to let the liquid in, are walls
the wetness and smooth edges crash against.
Nobody said this would be easy,
but let me pour another glass
half full of finer spirits and propose
a toast to the distant moment when
the muscles, having suffered much,
relax from their long ache, and the fingers
stop probing wounds and start to write
a few new laws of battle: though it's beautiful
to choke on fumes, it is better to breathe
pure air than noxious gases; there will come a time,
not soon but someday, when tragic figures
add up to comical sums; for every fall
there will be a spring; when the rumor goes
that all is lost, it is good to give large thanks
for little pleasures, foremost among them the fact
that the heart's response is a matter of
degree, not kind—whether the ax is lifted
in ardor or in fury, the frozen sea still melts.

A Turn for the Better

Strangely stable today, and a rain-slicked street
that once pierced me with its sorrow has turned
limpid and various as a view of Delft.
And the song I murmured yesterday—

> *Oh heart that aches*
> *and trust that breaks,*
> *for your poor sakes*
> *may all the charming flakes*
> *and no-good rakes*
> *be burned at spiked, enormous stakes*

has just revealed another verse—

> *The road is wide, is ravishing.*
> *Until I walk on solid ground*
> *no one is allowed to sweep me off it.*

Love and Work

In an uncurtained room across the way
a woman in a tight dress paints her lips
a deeper red, and sizes up her hips
for signs of ounces gained since yesterday.

She has a thoughtful and a clever face,
but she is also smart enough to know
the truth: however large the brain may grow,
the lashes and the earrings must keep pace.

Although I've spread my books in front of me
with a majestic air of *I'll show her*,
I'm much less confident than I'd prefer,
and now I've started pacing nervously.

I'm poring over theorems, tomes and tracts.
I'm getting ready for a heavy date
by staying up ridiculously late.
But a small voice advises, Face the facts:

go on this way and you'll soon come to harm.
The world's most famous scholars wander down
the most appalling alleyways in town,
a blond and busty airhead on each arm.

There is an inner motor known as lust
that makes a man of learning walk a mile
to gratify his raging senses, while
the woman he can talk to gathers dust.

A chilling vision of the years ahead
invades my thoughts, and widens like a stain:
a barren dance card and a teeming brain,
a crowded bookcase and an empty bed...

What if I compromised? I'd stay up late
to hone my elocutionary skills,
and at the crack of dawn I'd swallow pills
to calm my temper and control my weight,

but I just can't. Romantics, so far gone
they think their lovers live for wisdom, woo
by growing wiser; when I think of you
I find the nearest lamp and turn it on.

Great gods of longing, watch me as I work
and if I sprout a martyr's smarmy grin
please find some violent way to do me in;
I'm burning all these candles not to shirk

a night of passion, but to give that night
a richly textured backdrop when it comes.
The girl who gets up from her desk and dumbs
her discourse down has never seen the flight

of wide-eyed starlings from their shabby cage;
the fool whose love is truest is the one
who knows a lover's work is never done.
I'll call you when I've finished one more page.

Spring (The Procession)

after Joseph Stella

i.

And had it come to this?
All winter the leaves clung to the branches
and snow, withheld as an angry god's
or an old globe's accusation, never fell.
Fierce disorder followed: sleds languished;
sidewalks smelled of pine and lilac;
coats hung—dusty, comical—on high pegs.
White was a memory. And when spring came
it was only a name, a fact on a page
without the corresponding colors
that blared their message over town, shouting
You struggled through the cold, hard winter
now bloom on cue: be like me, be this green.

ii.

What could the downcast lovers of seasons do
but flee the warm city into springs
of their own making? And soon there were plenty:
false springs that came and went before breakfast;
strange springs that worried the downstairs neighbors;
fugitive springs that bad moods scared away.
But most of all there were lonely springs,
sudden flashes of insight that grandly promised
starlit gazebos and an end to hunger...
But the open window still opened on hunger
and the long street showed no sign of the mind's big day.

iii.

A thousand leaves rush forward:
bright, like an image of something lost,
quick, like a portent of something fast
becoming a page in a tear-stained book
that people look at in separate rooms, thinking
There was a thing called spring, and it gave
my better days a meaning. But now
that it's always spring, the days mean nothing;
the word's been bled of its earthy realness
and as the heat rises, to what in the world
can I ever compare my wildly leaping heart?

iv.

Down the various leaf-strewn paths we go,
she muttered sadly to her oldest friend,
the one she had walked with, arm in arm,
down all those broad alleys
through so many springs. He nodded, saying
We're on two roads now, heading away
from that marriage of reverie and green
too happy to last. Unless...Unless?
Unless, sitting in a ruined garden,
lost in distinctly chilly thoughts,
we sense traces of our favorite season
stirring around us, gathering weight and form:
I plan a punch line but you beat me to it;

a vagrant petal grazes first your arm, then mine;
a small bird lands on a stone bench and starts to sing.
When I stare down my narrow alley
a low voice says badness, madness, sadness;
but something happens when we look at the bird
and, looking together, invite it to stay.
A minute ago we were lost as winter
but now we're all headed in the same direction—
you, me, the bird, and this late spring day.

Lawyers on the Left Bank

So this is me at thirty-two, the strange dream seemed to say:
the lawyers order coffee in a louche Left Bank café
and read their menus carefully, and sit extremely still
while all around them lips kiss, fistfights rage, and glasses spill.
What they are doing in this rowdy tavern is not clear.
It's obvious they are not prudes, for after all, they're *here*.
But in this topsy-turvy room where tables serve as beds
and tarts are jumping out of cakes, what thoughts race through
their heads?
Perhaps they harbor fantasies of trading in their suits
for clingy leather bodices and sleek stiletto boots;
perhaps they scan the revelry and contemplate a fate
where working hard is not the solemn foe of playing late;
or maybe they just tease the air with legions of small sighs
and burn holes in the carpet with averted bedroom eyes.

Ruskin's Whip

John Ruskin—also me, in that odd way
two people share one body in a dream—
forced himself down a narrow flight of stairs
by whipping (one crack, one step) his own neck.
Then suddenly he stopped and hung his head,
too bloody and too weak to reach the street;
the trick he used to get himself ahead
had made another step impossible.
He sank into his frockcoat with a sigh:
his body and his brain refused to bid
each other farewell, and for all his pain
he wasn't even going up. Some stern
benevolent veiled spirit of the stairs
was giving warning, telling me there was
no going forward, but no turning back.

Sanity Clauses

If the carpet lifts and the sweepings fly up,

If butterflies, not just frogs, flee the unsealed jar,

If I start to see the bark on the trees in the dark, enormous forest,

If the loose screw tightens but does not rust,

If stressed leads backward to desserts and forward to feet,

If devils star in intermezzos not operas,

If the two huge totem poles shrink to a smaller, realer pair,

If shove comes to push but the pressure still presses,

If the dreams of barristers and banisters keep on coming,

If wearing my rue with a difference means focus, fury, not vanish,
                                                              anger,

If the bars on the windows become visible,

If daydreams are means not ends,

If the endlessly revolving door spits me out when I see the
                                                        waiting subway,

If the portrait of Pentheus falls off the wall and stays off,

If pleasure's antiphon's harder and harder to hear,

If I dance to the beat as well as the lyrics,

If the first lobster scene in *Annie Hall* remains my screwball
                                                              model,

If loving July does not mean cursing December,

If sphinxes relax but continue smiling,

If the Williamsburg Savings Bank becomes a friendly symbol,

If black blood turns lighter not thinner,

If the men in the war room take off their masks,

If pendulum souls stop taking me with them,

If ashes of dying stars reclump into new ones,

If "black and white and (say word!) all over" is a pun whose
                                           doubleness I savor,

If broken records mean medals not headaches,

If gin logic's if/then lasts past morning,

If the bats in the belfry still ask me to parties,

If I go to the circus and stare hard at the educated fleas and the
                                        second trapeze,

If the festering lilies don't spoil the meadow,

If Miss Havisham takes her dress to the cleaners,

If I like the letter scenes less than the waltzes,

If the speaking lion's a lifelong challenge,

If I get these silly lists out of my system,

If wide pores coexist with thick skin,

If early sorrows, forgotten but not gone, at last surrender to time's
passing,

If the sky's the limit but the ground suffices,

If I've circled the couch for revealing reasons,

If the trees on their traffic islands can still, fierce puppeteers, play
havoc with heartstrings,

Then take me and mend me; do all you want with my head.

Cures, Talking

You thought of Iceland,
how the sunlight, when it comes,
warrants the weight of the long darkness,
a starless dungeon becoming paradise.

You wandered in a forest of gauze
where bandages hid roots and treetops
but also gave you soft horizons,
no bats, and no bad weather.

You said the page was purge enough,
prized site of nightmares and denials
shaped into straight lines; spilling elsewhere
would squander effort and inhibit ink.

So when you knocked, and sat, and spoke,
we showed you a floodlit wood whose brightness
deepened the beauty of its branches,
we fondly smiled as you sketched our distant lodging.

Two Remedies

i.

RTW ache? Zen telos!

ii.

When that attempt at betterment—
Empty the mind I would not, could not—
Lasted about ten silly seconds
(Love's impossible, life's cruel, a voice
Boomed into the vacuum), I succumbed
Unwillingly as children creep to school
To the signed slip, the full bottle, and the
Really quite unanswerable question:
If I did recover, would that "I" be
No one I knew, or the true me back at last?

Listening to the Ocean

In a recent dream, I and a friend who
I couldn't recognize stared at a dam
breaking. My friend said, "What will happen to
the Pacific now?" Damp though I am
I won't have to find out; a giant wall
has come between me and the fiercely smarting
waters flooding me always, and lately all
my troubles reach me as trained sharks darting
in deep seas far away. Never mind
that the trendy capsule may be a thief
and not a restorer; never tell me a gloved hand
never wrote a good line. The waves were bad. And if
this false wall hides their horrors from my eyes
I'll swallow very gladly, and feel it rise.

The Mystery of Cigarettes

Some things intrigue me,
like how bands perform fadeouts
live, or why I smoke.

∾

I'm not a loser
because I'm alone; I just
needed a quick puff.

∾

Outlaw in a tie:
I have made a flame, and I
have snuffed it out, look.

∾

I love the way it
gives aimlessness an image:
minds drift, and so does smoke.

∾

An accessory
like pearls or tattoos, only
flickering, darting.

∾

Without one I'm all
thumbs: I blusteringly pose
or play with my hair.

Gracious sticks, many
thanks for giving me something
to do with my hands!

⁊

An urban romance?
You're one with the pollution,
soulmates with the smog.

⁊

Through this sultry haze
I lead a rich double life:
here and miles away.

⁊

"I must have one" and
"Ah, smoke in my hair" are twin
pleasures; between them,

strange disappointment
resides: all this fuss over
a mere cigarette!

⁊

Why do I buy one
pack at a time? To keep the
sexy guilt coming?

⁊

They become a kind
of timepiece: I will brood this
long, then back to work.

⁓

I'll quit tomorrow,
I'll quit next year—somehow the
constant deferral

comes to stand for all
the things I'm not ready for:
sound body, strong mind...

⁓

Some solitary
vices are just smokescreens for
facing true love's trials:

stub in one hand, scotch
in the other, I endure
such fire and water.

⁓

I know a man who
prefers second-hand smoke to
sampling the poison

for himself. I find
this fondness odd, like Chauncey
who would rather watch,

but maybe my friend
is onto something: he gets
all the atmosphere

without the danger,
all the pleasure without the
carnage or the cost.

❧

I had a vision
of organs turning black, and
so I puffed harder.

❧

Could the pack's warning
increase sales? "Others may die,
but I'll be different."

❧

A kind of comfort,
a brand of despair, that they
are always the same.

❧

It gets in your eyes;
debonair Camus's got one;
Bogart lights Bacall's...

Lovely metaphors,
bright narratives, while somewhere
old men coughed and coughed.

∾

Glamor of illness,
loosen your grip; I fear I've
got it all backward.

Simone Weil declared
true goodness—rather than bland,
workaday evil—

the most exciting
thing on earth. Perhaps as I
gaily inhaled I

gave health a bad name,
forgetting the much better
glamor of living!

∾

Little suicides,
rest in peace: I'd rather find
mystery elsewhere.

Four-Part Invention

A riderless horse has bolted from the stable,
explores the winter landscape with dark zeal
and all-night dances until something snaps,
snow mounts, and the rapture of the rupture
leads to a just plain bad break:
mouth afoam, and hoofprints on the moon.
Back to the awful door the poor horse creeps,
dreading the reigns of terror—docile dimness?
omnipotent evasions?—that await.
But it's strangely strange inside the stable walls;
a room in which you squint or flex
has more than its share of cold and weird and winter.
The warm horse stares the dust motes down,
seasons her oats with tiny flecks of foam.

Hello Yellow Brick Road

All that lazy summer,
degree in hand, I discovered cable;
the story of a foolish drummer
had me unpacking my turntable

and as Elton John's bassist bought
my old apartment, I danced in my new one
to songs my snug new self had long thought
banished with trial runs. Which was the true one?

Did I need to answer? There are more things
on heaven and earth...and all I knew
was that music from an open door brings
a welcome visit from a noisy crew

of past lives clamoring, *We're not dead
and we're not fatal. There's plenty of room in your head.*

Too Many French Movies

Too many French movies, and the air that was rich with the scent of primroses has grown sickly sweet overnight: I am bloated and faint from too many options; I sit in the darkness and whisper, *Commit, decide.* It is either time to move to Copenhagen, or to give some thought to forked roads closer to home. All the ravishing young things and their big dilemmas—will he marry the wild or the pious sister? which of the friends does she like better?—are melting into one beautiful golden blur. And the blur fades to black and the lights come back on. I sat and loved their summery problems, but now I crave the stark lines of winter, the charmless rigor of choosing wisely, all the things my old idol Marie avoids when she strolls in the gardens, a fair youth on each arm.

Madeleine for a While

after Hitchcock's Vertigo

Scottie looked down from a very great height,
and as Midge sat primly at her easel
he talked himself back into wholeness:
"I look up, I look down, I look up, I look..."

As Midge sat primly at her easel
he followed Madeleine through the city.
"I look up, I look down, I look up, I look..."
Down he fell all over again.

He followed Madeleine through the city;
the ghost of mad Carlotta steered her.
Down he fell all over again:
she jumped in the water and he jumped after.

The ghost of mad Carlotta steered her:
"There's someone within me, and she says I must die."
She jumped in the water and he jumped after;
they kissed in the shade of ancient sequoias.

"There's someone within me, and she says I must die."
Haunted Madeleine mounted the steps.
They kissed in the shade of ancient sequoias,
they parted when she leaped from the tower.

Haunted Madeleine mounted the steps;
Scottie pursued, obsessed and dizzy.
They parted when she leaped from the tower,
they met again in a crowded rush hour.

Scottie pursued, obsessed and dizzy.
An ill-lit corridor led to her room.
They met again in a crowded rush hour;
they argued in her fleabag hotel.

An ill-lit corridor led to her room;
Judy's dark hair confused the picture.
They argued in her fleabag hotel.
"Be Madeleine for a while," he begged.

Judy's dark hair confused the picture,
ruining the marvelous story.
"Be Madeleine for a while," he begged,
so she returned a dazzling blonde.

Ruining the marvelous story,
her necklace revealed all she had been
when she returned a dazzling blonde.
Holding Madeleine, he'd embraced air.

Her necklace revealed all she had been:
a stumble, a wail, a plunge into darkness.
Holding Madeleine, he'd embraced air.
One final thing and he would be free.

A stumble, a wail, a plunge into darkness.
He talked himself back into wholeness:
one final thing and he would be free.
Scottie looked down from a very great height.

A Day at the Revival House

The rose in Chaplin's mouth is always his;
when Nick Charles, pursing his lips, opines
"A dry martini you always shake
to waltz time," we don't strike his pose
though we'd love a little of his breezy charm.

But when Andre leans across the table
and whispers tales of burial alive,
at which Wally expresses baffled respect
but confesses *he's* just happy when
his coffee cup holds no cockroach in the morning;

when Isaac Davis quits his job
and flits from the adoring student
to the stern bluestocking and back again,
knowing he needs eggs but wondering
why the damn things crack so easily;

when Secaucus's Seven gather for
a weekend of charades and angels-
on-pins dissections of time's passing
(when do you finally stop saying
"What will I be when I grow up"?)

I'm in the restaurant, I'm buying eggs,
I'm one of their soul-searching crew
though the self that does the looking has changed
as often as their restless collective minds.
Meeting them for the first time, I loved

the romance of chaos: so this would be
adulthood in all its rich confusion!
The weeping fits on Manhattan streets,
the brilliant novel that can't get written,
even the lost ideals and savage breakups

were great ordeals I'd someday live through too.
Pre-shrunk, pre-lapse, I thought their dramas
prefigured my own glamorous traumas;
I couldn't wait to be a basketcase.
Such was moviegoing until,

first gray hairs discreetly dyed,
I arrived at the revival house and realized
I had become the talkative seeker,
I'd seen the strangled children of paralysis
by analysis and the fog-drenched

nowhere of muddles, I knew too well
the smell of spoiled eggs, the death of hearts
and the chilling moment when the soft veil lifts
and Poof! These are the eyes that were his pearls.
I watched the faces dance and flicker

and thought, in the grainy darkness, of
another metamorphosis in which
a butterfly longs for the cocoon—
terribly snug but strangely airy—
where it felt good to dream of butterflies.

Homage to Eddie Izzard

What vision lights up wildernesses tonight?
The sentry scratches his head and guesses tonight.

Too many diplomas! Their frames cast gloomy shadows.
She flees the dark room and regresses tonight.

The cats are drilling for oil behind the sofa;
the stage fills up with rich excesses tonight.

He did a show in perfect French in Paris.
Qu'est-ce que le mot juste pour *impresses* tonight?

The deity sounds strangely like James Mason,
for high and low exchange caresses tonight.

The shy commuters sit, lost in three-piece daydreams,
but this man practices what he professes tonight.

Bless me, father, for the man in makeup *moves* me,
the girl in the seventh row confesses tonight.

Do earwigs make chutney? Do spiders make gravy?
Is the hall enthralled by nonsense? Yes: his, tonight.

We'd grown too used to glamorous naysayers.
Only the final bow depresses tonight.

When I get home I'll place in the window
a candle lit for blokes in dresses tonight.

A Pre-Raphaelite Girlhood

Framed by russet curls, willowy as lilies
tended by the moon, she made bitter tears seem
so sublime that for a long time she was a
flattering mirror

into which I gazed, craving confirmation,
goals, reflections, rules: *I contain a world of
maladies too good for the world*, the canvas
sighed to me softly.

But that was before I compared corollas
of red hair and counted gray eyes and realized
They all look the same. Weakness has a power;
sorrowful maidens

haunt you, there's no way to deny it, with their
noli-me-tangere appeal; but when you
picture them on open-air walks, you sense they'd
melt in a minute.

Rows and rows of ravishing famished creatures,
swooning in Tate Galleries of the brain, still
lift their tragic arms to the waiting clouds and
tempt me to join them,

but I can't come—trudging down muddy roads, I'm
getting my feet dirty to clear my head, I'm
sunlit, breathless, looking for better ways of
looking in mirrors.

Rosalind in Manhattan

"So fare you well. I have left you commands."
—*As You Like It*, V.ii.118

i.

Let them feel a breeze and wonder,
is it you or the front door, opening?

ii.

Banish clichés only
to reinstate them as polished jewels:
love hurts, but you must not say it like that.
Cry "scarlet canyon."
Yell "wound supreme."
And in so doing, sew the wound up, count the jewels.

iii.

They have looked at you for so long
with stiff, unbroken gazes
that you've made—without even knowing it—
a splintered stare your own.
You've bounced from spotlight to stoplight.
Now practice a look that lingers:
on leerers, on lovers, on gutters,
on gargoyles. Gaze everywhere, gaze long.

iv.

When numb feet slap number pavements,
hum a few bars of "Rhapsody in Blue."

v.

Make creative leaps:
Straus Park as stageset for moonlit farce,
featuring...

vi.

Remember that there is banter and there is banter,
the cell phone's And-then-I-told-him
and the fugal antics of old friends
conspiring late in open-air badinage.

vii.

Watch crazy goals soar vertically,
like secular cathedrals careening skyward,
but meet them horizontally,
like sidewalks racing all around town.

Pemberley

The park was very large. We drove
for some time through a beautiful wood
until the wood ceased, and the house came into view.
Inside were miniatures, small faces
we gawked at until a housekeeper showed us
the master's finer portrait in an upper room.
I dredged up a shaming moment:
you asked me a question, then ducked as I spewed
an idiot's vitriol, blindness disguised as rage.
The house stood well on rising ground,
and beneath its slopes the thirsty couples
held their glasses high at Café Can't Wait.
I spent time at its flimsy tables
but then I walked under trees whose leaves
exhaled gusty stories of good deeds;
I learned empty houses are excellent teachers;
I sent you away and felt you grow
tremendous in your absence. Ask me again.

Short Ode to Screwball Women

On sullen nights like these
when my spirit counts its woes like pearls on a string,
you bring me armfuls of spare pantsuits
and clear-eyed hints about the woman
who might kick up her heels in them, flooding rooms
with cunning, air, an almost gaudy vitality.

Gaudy but sober: when your wayward husband
courted the heiress, you stormed her gates
disguised as a floozy—and asked the butler
to serve you gingerale. It was life
you'd rather be drunk on, roaring life
that told you there is no time for spirits
of dark staircases, only lightning ruses
that not only leave no bruises but give
all parties their wish: rinsed vision and second chances.

Losing a boot heel and giddily claiming
I was born on the side of a hill is easy.
For every such moment there are ten
when my ideal snags midflight, a bag caught in branches.
But a girl can dream, can realize, high
on heroines, that she is mortal
and therefore fearless; that sanity
supplies the ground bass to the wildest singing;
that breezes made visible make the finest winds.

On Leaving the Bachelorette Brunch

Because I gazed out the window at birds
doing backflips when the subject turned
to diamonds, because my eyes glazed over
with the slightly sleepy sheen your cake will wear,

never let it be said that I'd rather be
firing arrows at heart-shaped dartboards
or in a cave composing polyglot puns.
I crave, I long for transforming love

as surely as leaves need water and mouths seek bread.
But I also fear the colder changes
that lie in wait and threaten to turn
moons of honey to pools of molasses,

broad front porches to narrow back gardens,
and tight rings of friendship to flimsy things
that break when a gold band brightly implies
Leave early, go home, become one with the one

the world has told you to tend and treasure
above all others. You love, and that's good;
you are loved, that's superb; you will vanish
and reap some happy rewards. But look at the birds.

Down and Out in San Francisco

Granted, hills like hurdles dimple the city;
breezes like moods caress it and keep you guessing
nearness to bay. Slowly pull away
and beige, rose, yellow stipple the white,
but there will still be too much white,
and nowhere do the colors jitter,
go green-black-silver-brick, mirror
like they do back home my better days
and darkest moments. Hail fluctuation
in all its guises! Take me back
to where thunder claps in minds and skies
and hearts are glad to be unhappy! This lack
of seasons leaves me cold all over;
this bridge's broad smile is not, never was mine.

At the Zen Mountain Monastery

A double line of meditators sits
on mats, each one a human triangle.
Evacuate your mind of clutter now.
I do my best, squeezing the static and
the agony into a straight flat line,
but soon it soars and dips until my mind's
activity looks (you can take the girl...)
uncannily like the Manhattan skyline.
Observe your thoughts, then gently let them go.
I'm watching them all right, unruly dots
I not only can't part from but can't help
transforming into restless bodies—they're
no sooner being thought than sprouting limbs,
no longer motionless but striding proudly,
beautiful mental jukeboxes that play
their litanies of joy and woe each day
beneath the shadow of enormous buildings.
Desires are your jailers; set them free
and roam the hills, smiling archaically.
It's not a pretty picture, me amid
high alpine regions in my urban black,
huffing and puffing in the mountain air
and saying to myself, I'm trying but
it's hopeless; though the tortures of the damned
make waking difficult, they are my tortures;

I want them raucous and I want them near,
like howling pets I nonetheless adore
and holler adamant instructions to—
sprint, mad ambition! scavenge, hopeless love
that begs requital!—on our evening stroll
down Broadway and up West End Avenue.

292 Riverside Drive

for Julian Levinson and Lisa Makman

Each window holds a very different scene:
a spray of slender branches gives way to
a slightly wilder turbulence of green
beneath unequal quantities of blue.

But when a breeze stirs faintly on the left
a flurry can be noticed on the right
as these two landscapes, redefining theft,
keep borrowing and giving back all night.

Call it attunement or telepathy:
the way one square of world affects the other
yet still remains itself, this sympathy
that binds and complicates but does not smother

look like your marriage, and keep hope alive
for us who walk along the tree-lined drive.

The Long Run

Gregor's parents, after his tragic death,
traveled with their daughter out of the city
to a sunlit place where no one spoke of death.
How could he know how cruelly often death
invigorates the hard hearts left alive?
How could the soul die such an ugly death?
Grete, in a lewd affront to death,
sprang to her feet and stretched her fair young body;
her parents laughed like children; and everybody
savagely forgot the very death
that made them board the waiting tram and run
away from sickness as fast as they could run.

Such grisly stories plague me as I run
through Riverside Park months after my father's death.
Seasons have come and gone since my last run;
I scoff at types who "go out for a run"
come rain or shine; but suddenly the city
is glinting with green fields in which to run
my cares away, and so I'm on a run
this summer evening, feeling so alive
that even flecks of garbage seem alive
and my staid brain is quickly overrun
with more wild thoughts—hello there!—than one body
can act on. I am young; I have a body;

it has its needs; and how I wish somebody
would tell me why my scared thoughts used to run
from all the things I used to think nobody

could crave and still be civilized. My body
was what I'd gladly part with at my death
while my stern better half—mind, astral body,
spirit, soul, essence, whatever anybody
wanted to call it—lingered in the city
upholding proper standards in the city;
I'd live on as a potent antibody
against the basest element alive.
In those days I was only half alive.

But this new joy in simply being alive,
this tingling new awareness of my body
disturbs me. I'm the cruelest wretch alive
if you must die for me to feel alive
unless there is a reason for my run,
a need to keep your lust for life alive.
I won't believe I could not feel alive
until I'd watched your agonizing death,
but rather that the brute fact of your death
has taught me gratitude for being alive,
just as a nightmare of a ravaged city
reminds one of one's fierce love for that city.

A crowd of options chase me through the city.
I could stagger in sackcloth—barely alive,
grim as a reaper—through a stricken city
or I could cry, careening through the city,
it is a precious gift to have a body;
your memory is lighting up the city;

strange are the uses of adversity
if one man's downfall makes me want to run
and unlock all my locked doors, but I'll run
to all the well-paid sages in the city
until I grasp the unexpected death
of my skin's coldness brought on by your death.

My dearest father, I believed your death
would kill me too, but your beloved city
has never looked so glowingly alive;
your final breath still courses through my body,
inspiring every race I'll ever run.

Gusts

An agitation shakes the trees:
this tumult always seemed to me
the oldest motion, the turbulence
all others copied. As blossoms drift
down through the moist air, so blessings come
to those who wait long enough; when
pollen falls, the flight recalls
a fragile friendship dying. I never thought
that when petals touch the ground
the plenitude might stop there, the fragrance
be neither portent nor memory, but only
sweet smells lasting as long as the walk home.
It is spring; flowers are flying everywhere.
And all night a low voice chides me
for never giving my all to the moment;
a question forms and grows urgent
and won't take no answer for an answer:
if I gave up stories, what would become
of the gust, and the scatter, and the stillness after?
Would the trees be robbed of what made them priceless
or let their riches loose as never before?

Cloud Studies (I)

> "Let's cut out the transcendent twaddle when the whole
> thing is as plain as a sock in the jaw."
> —Wittgenstein

i.

But is it? Plain to *me*, maybe,
that when I walked into the sunset—
bent legs seeking the fleecy red region
where they might find rest—then swerved
and went on walking, I was choosing
the rigor of a difficult journey
over the fluffy myth of a happy end.

ii.

Yet others might have seen
a bad day's fiery funeral,
a good idea's vermilion applause,
a moment's blush extended over
the spires of upper Broadway. Twaddle dies hard.

iii.

To accumulate moisture is to let knives rust.
To look at clouds is to sharpen them again.

iv.

Crossing each street I saw
a grid made up of progress

(heading north, I was getting things done)
and gorgeous stasis
(in the west, above the park,
the violet streaks hung heavy, stayed long).

v.

A cigar is sometimes just a cigar,
but a cloud is never only a cloud.

vi.

Personality test: would you rather
be the water in the watertower
or the water in the cirrus, drifting east?

vii.

The clouds sail past the tall, strong buildings
like reckless racers, like foolish
featherlight notions. The buildings topple.
The balance alters. Now it is clouds that are strong.

viii.

Tumult of early morning:
the cloud resembled so many things—
a snowball, a glove, a crumpled sock,
a jutting jawbone—as the sun came up.

On Irony

> "The ironist is the vampire who has sucked the blood of the
> lover and while doing so has fanned him cool, lulled him to
> sleep, and tormented him with troubled dreams."
> —Kierkegaard

A verbal mitosis: one statement becoming two. With such swift multiplication the soul widens and the flesh rejects its limits.

A day without irony's it-might-be-otherwise moments, when you fly through the gap between *said* and *meant* to distant places, would be a horror: you'd feel your small heart ticking in a bare white room.

The woman who had been polite all morning, praising sun's rays and sad men's ties, found herself in a public restroom taking it all back: O scorching day, O lame cravats. It was not madness but the need for an alternate story, a flattened creature becoming round again.

But the birth of scare quotes caused problems for the lovers who spent the evening dodging the suspicion that their tryst had already happened. They "met in the café." They "exchanged meaningful glances." They "kissed in the moonlight." They wandered "home."

Meanwhile the words cried, Strengthen your feelings so these bars disappear, clean me, release me, say me like you mean me...

The obscure evil of the Hooters ad on 106th Street and Broadway in which a buxom blonde in skintight tee shirt looks up from her mug of beer as though the mug, the shirt, the world were the most ludicrous things ever dreamed up by man or beast. We may stare and summon outrage, but "Lighten up," the blonde seems to say. "Your fury is my self-knowledge. I am only an ad." She beats us to the punch. At which our rage and pity skitter into the night wind like all vain attempts.

Each statement spawned a rebuttal, each truth its own death, until the human shape grew obscured by—no, composed of—blades moving angrily in a downward spiral: Ironist Descending a Staircase.

The prince who saw camels and whales in clouds was not the singer whose hair turned another shade each year. There is a world of difference between a prism that gleams with many facets, and a series of masks beneath which there is no face.

Helping you flout the finite and skirt the simple, irony can be charming, a valuable skill at parties. But when the other guests recede behind a veil of words, it becomes tragic, and you become an audience of one.

Between the rock of "It was a special day" and the hard place of watching B movies all night I made my way...

And if irony is a burrowing inward, a bright light coming upon room after room in the mind's dark mansion, it meets its opposite in tears, the weary, beery relief of spilling your secrets and crying Out with it, I have burrowed long enough.

Dachshund

with apologies to D. H. Lawrence

What races through your head,
little sausage, fair lady of the hunt,
as you caper outside Janoff's Stationers, playing with your ball?

I do not know your name,
but if I asked your owners I would not be surprised
if the answer came back Lotte or Frieda.
Sweet Fraulein of Broadway!

In winter they dress you,
frisky precieuse, in clingy sweaters,
and in summer they give you free rein
of the sidewalk with its rich aromas.
Such sunlit liberty!

But when along strides the great dane
and spies you in your midday gambol,
your eyes become bright seething orbs;
your squat legs brace; you're ready for war.

Like long-ago mastiffs
you two grunt and spar on the sidewalk
as the little red ball heads toward the gutter
like the baby carriage bouncing down the Odessa steps.

Farewell to innocence,
darling sausage,

or rather hello to a heart you had all along,
beating wildly beneath your sweaters.

And I have something to learn from you:
a buried life.

Flaneur Haiku

To know my city
like a bold lover, to trace
its ravishing curves...

∽

I have tried tophats,
caps, berets, but I missed the
brisk air around me.

∽

Fair passing creature,
your quick step charms me more than
your clasp ever could.

∽

My imagined cape
billows in the frosty air,
snagging on nothing.

∽

Lovers holding hands:
a sign of sharpened senses
or stupefaction?

∽

Proudly alone but
craving one true companion:
passion's paradox.

❧

A plague on these phones
that invade and demean my
meditative space!

❧

When a woman falls
I do not stop to help her.
I was engaged, once.

❧

In the bright café
a crowd of flaneurs gather.
Away, foes, clichés!

❧

Never standing still:
I called it brave, but it looks
more and more like fear.

❧

Dark night of the soul,
can you be right when you say
I'm running away?

❧

Robed in mystery
I sweep through parks, through parades.
But cast no shadow!

❧

Never to be known:
charming as a beginning,
chilly at the end.

❧

Sunset's dark tatters:
beauty, mine for the taking
or hope, torn to shreds?

❧

The flesh is sad, and
there is nothing left to learn.
Walking helps, somewhat.

❧

When I stumbled home
the lights in the city paused
and went on shining.

Manhattan Triptych

i. *Café Pertutti*

Being here now be damned,
there is a motion in the passersby
that troubles comfort and brings on longing.
Midsummer evening, women drifting by

in peacock colors; what fitter thought
than *Watching them pass, I am happy?*
But summer is framed by ardent spring and dense autumn.
Where are they going in their emerald scarves?

ii. *Skater's Waltz*

This was the challenge: not to succumb,
that late gray afternoon in Port Authority,
to easy fury at the piped-in music—
such carefree, glittering sound must surround

much happier commutes than mine—
but to let the lushness pierce the grayness,
discover myself gliding in
an indoor rink with all the other skaters.

iii. *Grove Street*

Out on a limb, I liked the breezes
but feared the storms. Succeeding days
saw me stubbornly moving through crowds
with wide grin or vacant gaze—two sides

of the same page, for either way I was martini-dry,
incapable of bruising, noticing flecks on necks
rather than eyes, their daggers and their vistas.
And then a tree wept! The petals at my feet...

Largo

"Look for someone to make you slow."
—Elias Canetti

They are ogling the stars in an outdoor garden,
and the night's infectious energy
makes them bold, makes him grab her hands and declare
A brilliant chapter begins tonight:
I have novels in me, whole realms of feeling
your eyes prise open. To which she responds
I'm a changeling, darling, in your masterful hands;
this morning I was one of eight million stories
but now I'm wearing freshwater pearls
at the end of a pier, in the middle of summer—
race me there, and the waves will envy our speed.

A sudden hush descends over Café Largo
and a low voice whispers, Be all these things,
ring all these changes on each other
but slowly. The brain that races tonight
will end up a frowning skull in a viewless mansion;
you'll wake up in bare rooms, horrible jewels in your hands.
Walk, instead, past never-finished cathedrals;
light one cigarette from another;
find, if you know what's good for you, endless answers to whether
the table is really there when you close your eyes.

Commands for the End of Summer

i.

Deepen,
leaves, not with what
has made us sorry but
with what was profound about that
sorrow.

ii.

Make me
spontaneous,
gathering winds, but don't
blow so giddily I teeter
too much.

iii.

Songs I
listened to all
summer long, accept my
thanks: to regress is not to move
backward.

iv.

Splash of
patchouli on
my wrist, remind me that
in this cauldron there is a world
elsewhere.

v.

Smile! Those
days of humid
agony have earned you
the right to a hundred purple
sunsets.

vi.

Come, fall,
I can feel you
stirring, I can hardly
wait for the things that will happen
come fall.

Autumn Ghazal

I'm always inclined to brood on the first days of autumn,
roaming my neighborhood on the first days of autumn.

Shivering trees lined the streets where I wandered,
married to solitude on the first days of autumn.

All summer I swore I'd lost all hope—but there is no sight
sadder than a bitter prude on the first days of autumn.

The self I pieced together from a million *don'ts* and *cannots*
comes so wonderfully unglued on the first days of autumn.

All is fullness, ripeness, lushness. How badly I long to spill
the juices in which I've stewed on the first days of autumn!

I will go down the path the fallen leaves make, a carpet
inviting and crimson-hued, on the first days of autumn.

How fast my thoughts race on these gusty, raw evenings;
how fine to be wooed on the first days of autumn.

But for every new door the wind blows open,
an old fear is renewed on the first days of autumn.

Will the couples who fight through the long, harsh winter
be the same ones who billed and cooed on the first days of autumn?

Chilly hints of coming darkness—it's hard
not to feel nervous, subdued on the first days of autumn.

Mountains of snow will bury me soon enough;
let no more cold blasts intrude on the first days of autumn.

Even in this wild city, where frowns make such good armor,
we're all too thrilled to be rude on the first days of autumn.

Notes Toward a Theory of the Self

The lonely nomads fled their monads, looked around breathlessly at the constellations sailing past...

She paused from pining. That there was no going back was clear. But this restless intensity, this strange new desire to lick feet and prance in valleys—was she trying on a brand-new sequined suit, or noticing the one she'd worn all along?

To swallow or not to swallow the small blue pills: was the water without the waves still water? Would the willow trees sway less sweetly without the wind?

And along came cellphones, and "Where are you?" replaced "How are you?" Oh leave your troubles at home, so our crossed paths might create new ones!

Self as Tristan chord: always, if this aching music would resolve itself, there would be peace, there would plenty. But these things would also mean death. And so "I'll quit tomorrow," resolves the smoker and lights up; "This flirting is getting me nowhere," sighs the smitten girl, and lightly brushes her new friend's arm.

Patience and Fortitude turned in my nightmares into a cringing pair of cowardly lions.

I spent the morning attacking paperwork, each check signed meaning one more demon slain. But "Clair de Lune" came on the radio, woke them up and set them wailing again.

"Let me live to my sad self hereafter kind." But I'm lost without my precious wounds; scrape the welts away and there's no one left to be kind to.

Normalcy, normalcy, normalcy, the town crier's tiresome urging. But who loves a village without its idiot? Who seeks out its mazy, historical streets?

I bow to the blind man, but I also give thanks I can see. Which of us goes to bed that night?

Outside my window, Saint John the Divine at sunset: the crimson of shame, the charcoal of fear, the lavender of drowsy contentment. Like a crash course in Monet, or a portrait of my moods that hour.

Quite stoned, I lay on my bed and heard myself meow! But wait, it was my solemn cat looming above me. Or was it? Did I really want such permeable membranes?

And how, in love, could I really afford not to?

Marriage of, dark night of, vale of making…Scoff not: they're only metaphors, but they show us where we want to go.

I'm not a prude, I just like my presents intricately wrapped.

Anna Nigma wandered around town, worried: if she told her secrets, would she vanish that instant? If a schoolbus hit her, where would her mysteries go?

Idiot, slow down: the quick brown fox needs the lazy dog to be whole.

"You are beer in a champagne bottle," he told her, getting her absolutely right. "And you," she replied, "are champagne in a beer bottle. A toast to depths and surfaces and the lovely rare person who observes and stirs and disturbs them!"

As the weather is not the climate, the foul mood fell away; it cleared the gutters so the sun had more places to strike.

The first hint of rainfall sent her hurrying into the street. Let people talk: she couldn't pass up the chance to feel more herself than she had during that ghastly heatwave.

My state flower is a violet, but I wish it was a heliotrope.

"New York was his town, and it always would be." Indeed. But when I went away for the weekend and felt my molecules dissolving, I wondered whether my penchant for places was a bad, a harmful one.

A song I'd give my eye teeth to be able to sing someday: Oh my love, you have shown me it's never too late to learn the difference between a wall and a wall with a gate.

"Smile when you are ready," said the irritating fortune cookie. If it were as simple as that! For what, after all, was readiness? An especially fragrant autumn breeze? A clearing of the house or the head? A firm conclusion that everything mattered, or that nothing did?

The man with the stutter lost it when he lectured. But what happened during office hours?

"I cannot like what I look like unless you love me," said the foolishly honest girl. To which he replied, "I cannot love you unless I like what you look like." It was the saddest impasse ever.

His dreadful self-consciousness at the dance; her sinking feeling that she was kissing him badly; it was the gap between X and

"X" that caused all the trouble, that made performing so hard (notwithstanding the fact that there was no X).

Rose water, tobacco, and the sweetness of grass just after rainfall... If good moods were composite aromas, that would be their smell.

My ten-feet tall internal parents beat me like incompetent sadists: such nightmares of scale and timing!

Was it an iron fist in a velvet glove, or the other way around?

Once she imagined the voices inside her head as members of a circus. The humor and the pathos of the lion tamers, the high-wire acts, the clowns climbing out of tiny red cars! The phone rang three times; the vision was over.

He was lonely, unmoored. But when he made his strange proposal— all the first letters of a sentence, scribbled in chalk on the big oak table—she looked him straight in the eyes and whispered, "Y."

A morning prayer in cities: that the mask I wear for focus's sake, for safety's, falls off; that the face beneath does not quiver like Jello, but shimmers with health and life.

Alone or in company, immersed in cloud studies or crowd studies, my aim is the same: the thought caressed, the profile studied as though for the first time, habits unspooling in the generous dusk.

A body made of magic elastic; all manner of quirks inscribed in granite; a border solid enough to cross and come back to; at the end of the day I want so little.

Cloud Studies (II)

Calling crystal balls and prophets!
When soft hands have taught me pleasure
and hard work has brought control
will I sail through my days
in a jubilant haze,
the swings and shipwrecks gone where dead things go?

Not a chance. But not a good end either.
Struggle instead, dear moods, to resemble
the ideal cloud that passes by
and seizes vision with its union:
such a dream of textured water,
such fiery pinks, such deep and perfect blues.

A Trampoline in Wayne

September twelfth. Strange doings out at school:
two undergraduates are jumping on
a trampoline that's suddenly appeared
on campus. As the bustle of the day
gets underway (bells tolling; freshmen late
for chemistry; briefcases built for speed)
the girls bounce up and down as if the earth,
grown weary of the pain that makes it spin,
has stopped. Their motions grace a different world.

Whatever twist of fate has brought them here—
perhaps I'll open up the student paper
and read of some unorthodox class project
or learn the circus is in town—I watch
their fertile energy with stinging eyes
and think back to the chaos in Manhattan
(proud towers turned to Wheat Chex, autumn air
stinking of flesh and flame, downtown a wound
uptown gives blood to), and next thing I know
I'm telling stories, I'm inventing ways
the carefree girls are comments on the carnage:
however high we build our clever hopes,
some smiling villain sends them tumbling down
to smithereens. Or else, more happily:
though buildings are more fragile than we could
have guessed (one shape descends), our lust for life
(another rises) makes a foiled ghost of
each suicidal pilot who believes

we'll go down, scorched and beaten, with the towers;
when one strong healthy body crashes down
the other, just as strong, pops up again.

But these girls are adventurous; their leaps
are every bit as varied as their plummets,
and no trim definition—allegory,
parabola, plunge, surge, drop—holds them all.
There will be time for metaphor. For now
it is enough to watch them on this crisp,
peculiar morning and remember that
what's obvious is often what we need
reminding of: to be alive is to be
capable of jumping on a makeshift
trampoline in New Jersey for no reason;
though downcast moods like mine may fence them in,
people will keep inventing crazy schemes
and leaping high as long as there is blood
flooding their cheeks, fire burning in their eyes.

Henry Hudson Parkway Blues

> "Then it is not blue I see but myself seeing blue."
> —William Gass, *On Being Blue*

Late October; the days grew shorter;
cobalt shadows troubled the water,
and these first hints of darkness became—
for those whose blood inclines to black—
cause for lamenting, source also of joy.
The doomed girls weeping on rocks,
the haggard men in their outpatient bracelets
dotted the water's edge and looked their fill.

I too was hooked, could have sat for hours
watching as the waves' convulsions
churned up my passed vetoes and vetoed passes.
I could also have stared, with false, with passing rapture
at the turbulence roughing up the river
and said, Why then be sad? No anguish
if you are wakeful enough to feel the pain,

but genes or life won't have it: I brood easily.
I wooed blue, denied it, flailed absurdly
between the violence of bursting a grape
and the lie of leaving it on the plate
until wavering stopped, and a great weight lifted

when I realized how many kinds of blue
are out there—the smothering navy blanket,
granted, but also the ultramarine
enchanted water, the old moon's endlessly
expressive features. I let her rave;

I saw her dark moods deepen a river
I sank into like a cool bath, not a well.
Her cloudy trophies hang on my wall,
right next to the drawings I did as a child
of a fair-haired maiden, skipping below the sun.

Blue Octavo Haiku

after Kafka

In fat armchairs sat
indolence and impatience,
plotting my downfall.

༄

A wicked cage flew
across the long horizon
searching for a bird.

༄

I burned with love in
empty rooms, I sternly turned
knives within myself.

༄

"Behold the bright gate,"
the keeper said. "I am now
going to shut it."

༄

Hardly was the road
swept clean when ah! there appeared
new piles of dry leaves.

༄

But nothing could kill
a faith like a guillotine,
as heavy, as light.

❧

Happiness? Finding
your indestructible core;
leaving it alone.

❧

Into the heavens
flew a breathless legion of
impossible crows.

Indian Café

> "Even as children we soon recognize an intermediate category
> of items—dazzles, glints, shimmers, blurry edges—that we
> know are somehow products of an interaction between the
> objects, the light, and our visual apparatus."
> —Daniel Dennett, *Consciousness Explained*

It's a feast for the senses:
cumin and turmeric rise from plates,
sitars come to their cadenzas
and, just past the restaurant window,
moonlit figures hurry toward
what strange encounters bound to change
their lives forever? I want to know all.

But so much conspires against it—
the glints and blurred edges blinding me
to the passersby I try to see—
that like a cranky mirror-world Faust
I want to say, Vanish, dazzle, you are too thick;
you are making my study of faces very hard.

She's dumb as a post; he prowls
the demimonde looking (sad friend)
for answers...The casualties of blind love
and ignorant loathing drift like ghosts.
If I could see past the haze,
muffle the snap judgments, leave them
to their own plain stories, maybe we'd
begin to crave new chapters in
our narratives: a seat at the table,
long evenings trading drab fact
and spicy rumor, vindaloo for two.

Cloud Studies (III)

Enough, for now, of the willful invisible tendrils
that storm the sky and sculpt the clouds
into all the things I'm thinking of
as I wander up and down the tree-lined drive.
(I said *anima, animal, animus*
and they turned, my faithful shape-shifters,
into drifting souls, flying sheep, bulging cannonball sacks.)
No matter if noon's cumulus
becomes four o'clock's cumulonimbus;
I'm still not the one who's got the vapors.
(I cried out: how could I bear to add
the sky to my abandoners?
Then I loosened the reins and learned the facts:
nothing can hold this much water forever;
the letting go is the growing lighter.)
I opened my eyes, I wept like a cloud.

Thirty-Three

i.

In or out of the loop, I *was* the loop,
a shiny train set zooming around the room.

But like wind that loses itself in an alley
and is found, days later, turning upon itself,

like the woman who cries on her couch for an hour
then looks in a mirror and cries some more,

so moved is she by her own smeared features,
like the dream in which I was both judge

and applicant for a major prize,
self-reliance has an underside,

a silence that real storms, fierce tears,
strange dreams, with their rash explosions

rightly deride: oh break the stiff ring,
surprises I never saw coming, dismantle

and save me, lover the loop excluded,
sitting an acre, a table, a touch away.

ii.

There, there. Where, where? The murky girl I'd been
played havoc with the solid self I seemed,

and all at once a crowd of masked forms stationed
at a watercooler murmured a terrible cryptic chant:

your origin will be your terminus; your floor
will fill up with old lists and forgotten mantras;

your best and dearest plans of having
bare arms in summer, wild nights in winter

will feel the cold annulment of our curse.
You'll prove our prophecy with clockwork precision.

Where had they come from? What did they want from me?
If I could crush the crowd into one person

pointing an angry finger in my direction,
then bend the finger backward and plunge it

into the masked enchanter's awful heart,
I'd frolic in freshets, I'd flourish, I'd do such things!

iii.

I saw the tree, its branches frail as nerves,
and suddenly there came the urge to write

"I saw the tree, its branches frail as nerves."
Shared longings over coffee became a sonnet

on friends confessing oldest hopes and new fears
before the mugs were empty. And so I drifted,

Trigorin in jeans and pea coat, through long walks
and chance encounters, a scribe on the move,

an avid bee gathering pollen
from my own choicest flowers. Sweet honey filled

the honeycomb's small cells. But more and more
I plead with tree, I challenge mug to say whether

ambition shoots rays upon dim events
and makes them glow more brightly, or whether

this zeal's a dark cloud shrouding the city
each time I head out, craving its embrace.

iv.

Another winter, another glad romp down Broadway;
the knees and shoulders have blown away

and a mantle of transforming snow
descends upon the avenue. My season.

Like you I know the pleasures of concealment:
I bore the rose, I bore the silver rose

to my loved one's house, but kept it stowed
inside my frockcoat so the mirrors might show me

my own tight-lipped reflection, so violent, so silent.
Likewise to move among hoods and woolens

is to honor the noble art of keeping secrets.
Until the wind turns bitter, that is,

and a snowstorm of cold images
counsels against excessive love of winter:

a glassed-in blizzard raging on a desk top,
a silver coffin heaped with silver roses.

v.

"Trees think spring has arrived," the paper reported
that sad week that unseasonable heat lured

the buds out early—then killed the eager fools.
I am, I thought (myth-maker getting the better

of common reader), a Daphne with bad timing,
my leaves and limbs creating a hopeless tangle.

I talked a good game, but ask me for facts
and I'd ask to see the egress. I missed my father

unreasonably: grief fled, and then returned.
I studied hard and jogged often, proclaimed myself

ready for strange embraces, then stayed inside
shifting shapes, dusting corners, and sighing, I'm still not ready.

Thank goodness there are other trees left
to get my tips from, like these lovely ones

on their traffic island that shiver, startled
and awkward and grateful, the moment they feel wind.

vi.

At home or abroad, I scoured the landscape
for faces and things to grow testy over—

stormed like a scourge through Brighton Beach
seeing lumpy flesh in deckchairs and hissing

You are not Pierre, you are not Natasha;
wandered forlorn through Regent's Park recalling

another stroll a decade ago when I knew
I'd come back, not alone, spouting glad high talk

for which the old walk would have been trial run,
preparation, dimmest glimmer. What was I thinking?

People who live in a golden age
go around complaining of too much yellow;

if I stood anywhere truly sure or happy
my veiled eyes and marble feet would never move.

Yet still I haunt Broad Walk feeling restless,
search for waltzing shadows along the boardwalk...

vii.

The student smelled of smoke but knew no grammar.
The marathon runner, her big day over,

slumped in her subway seat like all the other
members of the rat race. Sad creatures

out of synch with themselves! Long years
of living like them, reach giving grasp

a run for its money, rapid aims always beating
tortoise-slow attainments! Until somehow

the tortoise caught up, and I arrived
at a version of myself more stone than water.

But keep the cardigans away, I'm looking
for brand new ways of being lopsided:

I will water all my plants with seltzer,
I will paint my nails blue on alternate Mondays,

I will learn the latest racy dance steps,
though the floor beneath me gleams with bright hard wood.

viii.

Morning; who's there; the wish to be Irene Dunne
collides with the urge to head back to bed,

solemn brain solemnly dreaming. Morning induces
a delicate truce, but all the long day,

at work and at play, the battle continues:
travel light, armed with quips and cute hats,

chasing errant leopards through Connecticut,
or travel heavy, clothes black, outlook black

as the whirling world's inscrutable center?
Both have their beauties. But I choose lightness.

To warble of cottages small by waterfalls
is to wipe away the grime from seen-it-all windows

and light can always make room for darkness
though darkness lacks the strength to let in light.

The screwball heroine paused in her singing to realize
awful truths, then took up her song again.

ix.

When you've drunk too much, time garbles just like speech.
I'm sipping here, sitting my scotch and thinking

of the stories I'll tell with thirty-three more years behind me:
how I finally quit my band, the Repercussions

and formed a new one, the Gem-like Flames
whose soulful lyrics even critics loved.

How I sold the house where I grew up,
dark palace of cloakroom wit and armchair courage,

and only stayed in places which obeyed
the following rules: lawn as large as garden,

zero carpets, bookcases with lived-in look.
How noted film star, Teri Dactyl, wanted to buy

the rights to the saga of my life
and how I refused—I wasn't done with it yet.

By now I'm wording my slurs and getting sleepy,
but thirty-three years on, ah the stories I'll tell.

x.

In another story it would end like this:
when the heart grew weak from too many lashings,

when the soulmates vanished or disappointed,
she took off for a penthouse greenhouse

where lilies danced in a fan's warm breezes
and nothing could touch her. And sure enough

nothing did: not her unborn blushes,
let alone guests from the cold, with their glad red faces.

Her greenhouse turned green with clippings. But then
one night, sipping strong mint tea, she remembered

the stir a branch makes when spring rain bends it,
how it dips and veers in joy, in fear, for dear life.

The splendor of all her wounds waiting to happen
entered her, and she wrote a story:

"I summon hunger and risk, those lovely
scattershot graces," was the way it began.

Sakura Park

The park admits the wind,
the petals lift and scatter

like versions of myself I was on the verge
of becoming; and ten years on

and ten blocks down I still can't tell
whether this dispersal resembles

a fist unclenching or waving goodbye.
But the petals scatter faster,

seeking the rose, the cigarette vendor,
and at least I've got by pumping heart

some rules of conduct: refuse to choose
between turning pages and turning heads

though the stubborn dine alone. Get over
"getting over": dark clouds don't fade

but drift with ever deeper colors.
Give up on rooted happiness

(the stolid trees on fire!) and sweet reprieve
(a poor park but my own) will follow.

There is still a chance the empty gazebo
will draw crowds from the greater world.

And meanwhile, meanwhile's far from nothing:
the humming moment, the rustle of cherry trees.

Rachel Wetzsteon is the author of two previous poetry collections, *The Other Stars* and *Home and Away,* and a book of criticism about W. H. Auden, *Influential Ghosts: A Study of Auden's Sources.* Her poems regularly appear in leading magazines and journals, among them *The Nation, The New Republic, The New Yorker, The Paris Review, Poetry, Raritan, Salmagundi,* and *The Yale Review.* In 2001, Wetzsteon was the recipient of the Witter Bynner Prize for Poetry from the American Academy of Arts and Letters. She teaches at William Paterson University in New Jersey and the Unterberg Poetry Center of the 92nd Street Y, and lives near Sakura Park in New York City's Morningside Heights.